IMAGES OF ENGLAND

Withernsea

IMAGES OF ENGLAND

Withernsea

Mave & Ben Chapman

NONSUCH

For Heather and Dan whose caring support has given us both
the faith to 'hold on to our dreams'

First published 1996
This new pocket edition 2006
Images unchanged from first edition

Nonsuch Publishing Limited
The Mill, Brimscombe Port,
Stroud, Gloucestershire, GL5 2QG
www.nonsuch-publishing.com

Nonsuch Publishing is an imprint of Tempus Publishing Group

British Library Cataloguing in Publication Data.
A catalogue record for this book is available from the British Library.

ISBN 1 84588 339 X

Typesetting and origination by Nonsuch Publishing Limited
Printed in Great Britain by Oaklands Book Services Limited

Contents

Acknowledgements

We would like to thank all the many people who have been kind enough to talk to us and share their memories of the town and its activities over the years, some of whom wish to remain anonymous. We would particularly like to thank Molly Lawton for her kind help and encouragement, and for sharing with us her vast local knowledge. Also Wayne Wolton for practical help and interest. The following people have also proved of great help to this publication: Mary Blenkin of Ryehill, Mrs. Lillian Fussey of Patrington, Tom Graham of Easington, Ron Grayson of Bilton, Mrs. Kitty Griggs of Withernsea, Miss Irene Lawson BEM of Withernsea, Steve Lunn of Withernsea, George and Gladys Lyon of Withernsea, Miss Eileen Saunders of Withernsea and Mrs. Betty Wright of Withernsea. Withernsea Library and the Hull Reference Library have both been helpful with research material. All reasonable attempts have been made to trace owners of copyright where applicable.

Introduction

The earliest record of Withernsea dates from the reign of Edward the Confessor (1047-66). At that time it bore the name Whithornsea, which is said to mean 'whitethorn by the water'. The present town now lies in two ancient parishes, Hollym at the south end and Owthorne at the north. In its early days it came under the jurisdiction of such colourful characters as Tostig, Earl of Northumberland and the infamous Drogo. Withernsea, like most of Holderness is based on boulder clay. There is a long record of constant erosion, with many villages in the surrounding area already being taken by the hungry sea, which continues up to the present day.

In the year 1444 the village of Withernsea, which was at the seaward side of the parish of Hollym, was largely washed away. Owthorne which was at the north side of the original village of Withernsea was to suffer a similar fate at a later date.

The few remaining people, with great courage, continued to till the land, and in 1488 a new church was begun on the site of the present St. Nicholas Church. It is also thought that at this period, the mere, which was in the area of the present Valley Gardens was breached and claimed by the sea. At certain times in the year when there are extremely low tides, deposits can be seen on the beach which are said to be the site of the old mere. To skip the centuries and take a brief look at the nineteenth century, more erosion took Owthorne Church and part of the graveyard. The beach became a paradise for graverobbers, as coffins and corpses were exposed and scattered. Tales are also told of plundered wrecks as the sea took its toll of unseaworthy vessels.

In the mid nineteenth century fishermen began to ply their trade from the town; some families came up from Norfolk bringing their traditional boats to vie with the local cobbles.

It was during this period, with the advent of the railway that Withernsea really came into its own. This also coincided with a rising interest in the seaside, and the benefits to health which it allegedly provided. At this point in its development we begin to illustrate and relate the story of Withernsea and its people.

The town grew, as building programmes were undertaken, including inns and hotels. Facilities were provided, both for the enjoyment of visitors and residents over the latter part of the nineteenth and the early years of the twentieth century.

With its new railway link the town became almost a suburb of nearby Kingston Upon Hull. Commuters were conveyed to work in Hull, but more important for the prosperity of Withernsea, were the hordes of day trippers who made the return journey to enjoy the amenities during the summer season. Many of the families who came to the resort year after year often stayed in the same accommodation, thus forging links with the local people. It is fair to say that Withernsea as a resort and town exists due to the efforts of Anthony Bannister. He could be described as an entrepreneur who possessed a forceful personality. Bannister was a merchant and ship owner in Hull, and from 1845, when he became councillor for North Myton Ward, played a useful part in local politics. By 1851 he had become Sheriff of Hull, and it was in 1852 that he conceived the idea of the Hull and Holderness Railway Company. By this time he was Mayor of Hull. He was then 37 years of age and considered by his contemporaries to be very young to have achieved so much.

Bannister was far sighted enough to realise that the railway could be invaluable for the transport of the needs of agriculture between the villages, and the movement of freight between Hull and Withernsea. He also had the vision to realise the possibility of building up the town into the popular resort it was to become, thereby ensuring the profitable passenger traffic.

The opening on the 20 June 1854 was a huge success in spite of both wind and rain. Village stations were bedecked with the usual bunting and the church bells at Hedon were ringing a welcoming peal as the train approached. Anthony Bannister also decided there should be a hotel which could provide for the needs of the discerning visitor to the town, and so the Hull and Holderness Railway Company built the Queen's Hotel in close proximity to the railway station.

The hotel's opening ball was a very grand affair which included the first performance of the Withernsea Quadrille by the Hull musician Enderby Jackson. Bannister then became an Alderman. In 1862 the railway became part of the North Eastern Railway Company as the growth of the resort had proved disappointingly slow, and the Queen's Hotel was offered for sale in 1892, and became a convalescent home.

Sir James and Mr. Francis Reckitt bought the hotel with the idea of providing accommodation for the poor people of Hull, where, as in many cities tuberculosis (or consumption as it was then called) was rife. It was ideally situated to fill the condition of fresh air as prescribed by the physicians of the day as being essential to aid recovery. There were also facilities for people recovering from other serious illnesses. In 1902 the Reckitts presented it to Hull Royal Infirmary. The building is still used today providing among other medical services, beds for convalescing patients. Bannister began to give serious thought to building up the town. His early plans were for the north end of town, the first streets being the Esplanade which was later renamed Bannister Street in his honour, Young Street, Edward and Arthur Streets.

He was also involved in the building of the ill fated pier and also the North Promenade. Fortunately he was not to know the tragedy of the pier, as he witnessed the opening in 1877, but died in the July the following year. Credit is certainly due to his foresight as his schemes which began the development of the town were the basis for others to follow. The features of the town which remain as a reminder to people of his ambitions are the Hospital, Pier Towers, the North Promenade and Bannister Street.

Withernsea never really aspired to the reputations of seaside towns further north like Bridlington or Scarborough, rather has it fostered an image of friendliness and family holidays in an almost classless atmosphere. It built its reputation on its sweeping sandy beaches and bracing air, guaranteed to be beneficial to all.

In the pre-railway days, the tiny population of the town, around 125 souls, were predominantly engaged in agriculture. There was of course a grocer, a shoemaker, and the ubiquitous publican. The town was isolated and any journey which had to be taken of necessity, for the sake of the animals or to sell produce, was made on foot, sometimes leading a horse and cart, but more often just tramping along the primitive roads. There are accounts of people regularly making journeys to Hull in this manner.

By 1861 the population had grown and a wide diversity of occupations were listed in the census of that year. There were now people employed in various capacities by the railway company, there was a police constable, a draper, a tailor, and those employed in the catering services for the seasonal visitors.

The striking feature of Withernsea, as compared to many towns, is that there has never been any area which could be designated as a slum. Because of its character, which as already stated, was basically agrarian, and latterly orientated towards the holidaymaker, the buildings reflected the type of person who was catered for. Heavy industry with all its disadvantages, such as poor quality housing and densely populated areas were never features of Withernsea, a major factor which adds to the charm of this unique little seaside resort, which lifts it above some of the more affluent places in Yorkshire.

It is a long narrow town which virtually hugs the coastline, and in spite of recent changes, a town with a predominantly Victorian and Edwardian character, and the same friendly atmosphere which in earlier years ensured its popularity.

During the last war, there was a German air raid on Withernsea. Many Hull people, a city more heavily bombed for its size than any other place in England, including London, came to Withernsea for respite from the horrors of the blitz. Some to stay permanently, others just for a little peace and quiet before having to return to face the ordeal.

Many older residents speak with respect of the courage shown by these visitors, some of whom had lost everything including their homes, and in many cases loved ones. They came to Withernsea with the knowledge that a few days of relative peace and quiet would bolster them for the trying times ahead.

Concerts were organised and funds raised at the time, both for the relief of the Blitz victims and comforts for the local men and women serving in the armed forces. People rallied round to give support wherever they could, there was a great camaraderie and an overwhelming warmth and friendliness which has been typical of Withernsea throughout the years.

The ensuing pages give an insight into some of the people who left their mark on the town, and events which have shaped its destiny over the years. This is a book about Withernsea with a difference.

The people featured are from different backgrounds, from entertainers to educators, but all stamped their philosophy, or endeared themselves both to visitors and residents in their individual ways.

We have attempted to convey the development of the town and some of the events which changed it for better or for worse.

When the Hull to Withernsea railway line fell foul to the Beeching Axe in 1964, it was a body blow to the town, but with the spirit that has pervaded over the years, Withernsea has managed to remain a lively and thriving town, still drawing many visitors during the holiday season, and bringing in hordes of visitors to its impressive Sunday Market.

Coastal erosion has again raised its ugly head, and extensive repair work is currently in progress to fortify the North Promenade, after a terrible battering from the waves of the equinoxal tides over the last couple of years. There is also a lively regeneration scheme being organised which included a visit by His Royal Highness the Prince of Wales to view the town in the June of 1995.

This is the town of Withernsea. In some ways very little has changed over the years, still remaining are some of the characteristics envisaged by the far sighted Anthony Bannister, aided by his committee.

The present day outlook of the residents still cherishes the past, but looks forward into the future, a future which will bring a new population of visitors to the town each summer season.

One

Beginnings and Development

Every seaside town had a composite view card. This one from the early 1920s, shows the attractions of the town in a carefully selected group of vignettes, with the hope of catching the attention of the recipient, and attracting another prospective visitor. This practice still pervades though today's postcards tend to be garish and brightly coloured with little of the charm of their predecessors.

The train arrives at Withernsea Station. This obviously was a commuter train, the disembarking passengers being mainly gentlemen clad in the type of clothes considered suitable for business. The impressive building is the Convalescent Home, which as stated in the introduction was originally built as a prestige hotel. When the Queens opened 1855 it contained many bedrooms, bathrooms, a dance saloon and tastefully laid out gardens. As can be seen, it is a spacious three storey building which lent itself admirably to the conversion.

Opposite above: A very different picture! Compare this to the previous illustration. The trippers, or as they were colloquially referred to 'comforts', a corruption of the Yorkshire phrase 'come for t'day' were the people who brought the real prosperity to the town. This scene is by no means unusual, trippers coming in their hordes from Hull and the surrounding villages. A very mixed company, showing all types of dress from bowler hat to flat cap and muffler, and all ages from small children to the older generation.

Opposite below: The Convalescent Home seen from the railway station. The advertising on the station is interesting with things as diverse as Crossley's Gas Engines and Waterloo Cakes.

CONVALESCENT HOME — WITHERNSEA.

Florence Mary Scott Cavell, sister of the celebrated heroine Edith Cavell who was executed by the Germans during the First World War, was born in 1867 to the Reverend Frederick, and his wife Sophia Louisa Cavell, at the village of Swardeston, which is five miles south of Norwich. They lived in a red brick Georgian house which later became known as Cavell House. Like her sister, Florence became a nurse and was Matron of Withernsea Convalescent Home and Hospital from 1913 to 1945. Her gravestone in the adjacent St Nicholas churchyard records that she died on 2 June 1950. There are many stories about Matron Cavell. She appears to have been well respected and some older residents in the town still have fond memories of her. One rather interesting story is that every evening she made her rounds carrying a lamp in true Florence Nightingale fashion, one of our informants remarked that this had rather an eerie effect when viewed from Queen Street.

Sanatorium Station

Above: The Sanatorium which was added to the Convalescent Home in 1902. The beds on the balconies ensure that TB (tuberculosis) patients received the rest and plenty of fresh air which were deemed imperative for their recovery.

Right: The balcony beds at the Convalescent Home, with patients taking advantage of the clean fresh air. It was taken in 1916 and the photograph shows some men in uniform, it is not clear if they were hospital patients or visitors.

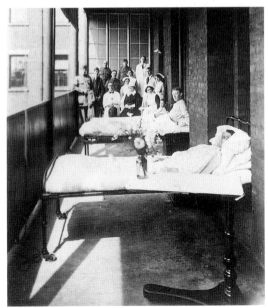

An interesting group assembled at the Convalescent Home in December 1910. It has been suggested that they were staff and their families, rather than patients. Even the hospital cat has managed to get his picture taken being firmly held by the nurse in the centre.

A very early picture of Young Street taken in the latter part of the nineteenth century. The first houses to be built can be seen to the right of the picture. This is before the bandstand was erected, and gives one a clear view of the sea. The street took its name from James Young who was Chairman of the Withernsea Improvement Company.

A much different view of Young Street taken around 1912. The Bandstand can clearly be seen on the Promenade. Apart from the fact that the Bandstand has now gone, and the cast iron railings were removed for the war effort during the last war, the scene has not changed at all to this day. The couple on the right, are standing outside the house of the writers of this book.

This is Queen Street, north end around 1904 looking towards the town centre. the imposing church spire is that of the Wesleyan Church which was built in 1900 on the corner of Queen Street and Young Street, the builder being W.N. Carr. Sadly the church was demolished in 1961 and Withernsea was the poorer architecturally speaking, for it was a truly magnificent building. On the site accommodation for the elderly was built and named Wesley Court. The striking feature of this photograph is the lack of traffic on the metalled road. There is a conveyance taking people into town and also a cart laden with sacks coming in the opposite direction, possibly a carrier or coalman.

A very old picture of the original Butterfly Inn on Queen Street. The present hostelry is much larger and more impressive. The Butterfly was opened in 1892 during a period of enthusiasm by the planners who were trying to provide amenities and accommodation which could attract more visitors to the town. The almost derelict cottages belong to an earlier period before the advent of the railway when Withernsea and Owthorne were basically rural agricultural areas.

A troup of militia parading down Queen Street. The men appear to be taking a greater interest than the women, having paused by the kerbside to watch the soldiers pass. The building to the left is the Alexandra Hotel which was built in 1871. It stood in both parishes of Owthorne and Withernsea which finally became a single Urban District, with a council in 1898. The building which originally stood on this site was a large thatched house known as Got and Gate House. This is thought to derive from the right of pasture for grazing cattle which was let to cottagers in the summer, and 'gote' which is the word for a stream derived from Norse origins. The road through Owthorne and Withernsea is said to have crossed this waterway in the area of the boundary.

An interesting picture of Queen Street early in the twentieth century which admirably illustrates the leisurely way of life. There are numerous shops, including Metcalfes's Tobacconist, Chamberlin and Teasdale with a newspaper rack. On the corner is F. Piper's shop with a display of clothing, and the Victoria Cafe. The lady standing near the doorway close to the horse and cart is thought to be one Miss Otis. The mode of transport appears to have been the bicycle; not a car in sight.

An early picture of the front of Brown's Central Supply Stores taken in the early part of this century. Every inch of space which could display goods has been utilized to the full extent, even the first floor windows.

THIS WEEK'S SPECIAL OFFER

———

1 TIN of PEARS
And a Tin of Rich Thick Cream
for **1/-.**

———

1 lb. of GOOD TEA
And 2 lbs. Best Granulated Sugar
for **1/9.**

———

BROWN'S
Central Supply Stores, Ltd.,
WITHERNSEA.

Brown's Central Supply Stores on Queen Street had a high reputation. Over the years this became well established until in the 1920s the signs above the fascia declared them 'Servants of the Customer' and 'Provision Merchants, Grocers and Tea Dealers'. The accompanying advertisement was placed in the local newspaper in 1929 showing prices of special offers, which in comparison to today's economy are really startling. To the right of the picture in front of Chapman's Boot and Shoe Shop is the Jubilee Lamp which was erected to commemorate Queen Victoria's Diamond Jubilee. The lamp was later moved to facilitate the smoother passage of traffic.

Opposite above: When it became apparent that the original Queen's Hotel beside the railway station was not reaching the commercial expectations of the North Eastern Railway, it was sold as previously stated and became a convalescent home. A new but smaller Queen's Hotel was built on Queen Street, south, between 1898 and 1901. Over the years many functions have taken place in this spacious, well appointed building. In 1935 a dance hall was built on the Cheverton Avenue side of the hotel.

Opposite below: The houses built in Withernsea in the late nineteenth and early twentieth centuries were mostly two storey terrace houses, built in either red or yellow brick. There were also a few three storey houses and houses with attics. Princes Avenue (originally named Princess Avenue) was one of the earlier streets to be built, and Eaton Villas are a good example of the bay windowed terraces of the period. It is enhanced by the corner house with the balcony of wrought iron around the imposing second floor bay window with the slated steeple on top.

QUEENS HOTEL WITHERNSEA

Eaton Villas, Hollym Road.

Seaside Road, Withernsea.

Cheverton Avenue was named after Martin Cheverton Brown. He was a wealthy financier and took a great deal of interest in the town. He was four times Chairman of Withernsea's Council and it is his house which is now the town's Municipal Buildings, the grounds of which became the Italian Gardens. The horse drawn cart with the white aproned delivery man belonged to William Cussons Ltd of Queen Street. The firm were high class provision merchants who were universally respected for their courtesy.

Opposite above: An interesting view of what is described as Station Crescent. The Police Station is on the left with the railings on the wall, and it is now known as Railway Crescent. The mounted rider and his dog are the only 'traffic' down this quiet street.

Opposite below: Seaside Road looking west. The tower of the lighthouse dominates the skyline. Though only a very short street, which as its name implies, joins Queen Street and the Promenade, it has had its share of drama over the years. In 1913 both the Assembly Rooms and the Council Offices were destroyed by fire. There was a post house for the lifeboat from 1881 until 1913, and also for a time a Fire Station. The street today is rather similar, with the Pier Hotel on the right still in use, and on the left a series of small businesses and cafes. The site of the boat house is now an amusement park.

Queen's Terrace with its imposing houses and a communal garden in the front. The large house on the right was that of Mr. Martin Cheverton Brown, and is now the Municipal Offices. The maritime statue has now gone and in its place stands the Jubilee Lamp.

Council Offices were built on Seaside Road in 1908. At the official opening on 9 March the town worthies gathered, those seated on the front row are said to be Mr and Mrs C.H. Lockey, and Mr and Mrs Cheverton Brown. The gentleman standing next to the lady in furs on the extreme right of the photograph is Mr George Cammidge. Sadly the building was destroyed by fire in 1913 and for a time the council met at premises in Bannister Street. In 1922 the current Council Offices on Queens Terrace, Queen Street South were bought for the Council.

"HULL TIMES" WEEKLY CARTOON

WITHERNSEA PIERROTS

KRUGER THERE'S HAIR!

MATILDA

LONE AND HEAR WHEN WE ARE MARRIED ON THE MEGAPHONE

SKINS

HOST AND HOSTESS

Mr CHEVERTON-BROWN'S GARDEN FETE AT WITHERNSEA.
Thursday, August 30th, in aid of the Port of Hull Sailors' Orphan Homes.
Some Sketches at the Garden Fete, by one of our Special Artists.

In the year 1900, the *Hull Times* published what they referred to as the weekly cartoon, which very often related to local social events. This cartoon depicts the Garden Fete held by Mr. Cheverton Brown and his wife on 30 August of that year in aid of the Port of Hull Sailors Orphan Homes, in their spacious gardens in Withernsea. The host and hostess are characterised along with some of the entertainers including a pierrot. The reference to Kruger, the Boer statesman who started the second Boer War (1899-1902) is of course, intended to be derogatory. A popular figure of fun and derision, at this period his effigy was often a substitute for Guy Fawkes on 5 November bonfires.

An aerial view of Withernsea looking south. Apart from the lighthouse at the top of the photograph, other present landmarks are St. Nicholas Church, the Convalescent Home and the Railway Station.

AERIAL VIEW OF WITHERNSEA. (90.010)

A similar aerial view of Withernsea looking north towards Waxholme. Note the many fields around the town which give some indication of its still rural surroundings. The lighthouse, to be seen at the top left of the photograph, adjoins fields which are now given over to housing.

This tower of an old windmill is known variously as Waxholme Mill, Withernsea Mill and the Black Mill, although strictly speaking it is situated in the old manor of Owthorne, and it should be designated Owthorne Mill. The first mill recorded on the site was in the fourteenth century. This mill last produced flour in January 1892 and the building was still intact but minus the sails in 1904. During the 1914-18 War the mill and grain store were used by the army. All that now remains is a short stump of the tower.

North Cliffe Farm, as the name implies, was situated at the north end of the town. The traveller who wished to go to Roos or further afield in that direction had to pay a toll to pass through the farmyard. It is recorded that in the early part of the twentieth century it was still possible to drive round between the edge of the cliff and the farm buildings, but before the First World War this had become impossible due to erosion. The last family to work the farm until it finally disappeared into the sea, were the Lyons family.

Two

A Walk Beside the Sea

In 1948 it was decided that Withernsea should have its own symbol. It was intended that everything printed appertaining to the town should bear the symbol. Tradespeople were asked to incorporate it on their stationery and business cards. There was a competition and a design submitted by Mr. H. Blackbourne of the Butchers Department of the Hull Cooperative Society's branch in Withernsea, was chosen. The design was eventually amended. The child with bucket and spade was redrawn to make the age more suitable and rays were added to the sun. The second image was considered more lively and inviting.

Band Stand and Promenade, Withernsea.

PARADE, WITHERNSEA.
WOOLASS SERIES No 21.

Right: Enjoying the sun near the Bandstand. One adventurous little girl has climbed onto the balcony as a good vantage point for looking out to sea.

The Promenade, Withernsea

Opposite above: The Bandstand which was built in 1901 was a popular amenity in the town. Situated on the North Promenade at the end of Young Street, it drew crowds of people to the open air band concerts. Sadly it no longer exists. The steps to the left of the picture gave access to the beach, these were replaced with stone steps, at this moment, workmen have removed them altogether in the current work on the new sea wall.

Opposite below: This peaceful scene of the North Promenade was taken in the vicinity of the Coastguard Station in 1905. During the Second World War, an anti-aircraft gun was mounted on the curved promontory. Until recently the scene has little changed, but due to the problems of coastal erosion, which has apparently undermined the structure, it has been removed as part of the new protection scheme. The North Promenade is being fortified by the tipping of thousands of tons of granite rock and the rebuilding of the sea wall at an increased height for extra protection to the town.

North Promenade pictured around 1909. It would appear to be typical Withernsea weather as the ladies are hanging onto their hats. The town is accustomed to sharp breezes, indeed it is said that for that reason the town was considered an ideal setting for a convalescent home. Apart from the mode of dress, the scene has changed little since 1909.

Quite an unusual photograph of two children riding donkeys along the road of the North Promenade in the 1950s. The donkeys, led by their owner, are probably on their way down to the beach. The scene has little changed, the only anomaly being the complete absence of cars, due to the 'No Parking' sign.

The South Promenade around the turn of the twentieth century as viewed from the vicinity of the Pier Entrance.

A very early picture of the Pier Entrance showing part of the actual Pier platform before it was finally dismantled in 1910.

This picture of the Pier entrance was taken around 1907. During the first decade of the twentieth century only about fifty feet of the pier remained. The 'Gate' with its impressive flight of steps soon became the venue for alfresco entertainment, and a favourite pitch for Catlin's Pierrots. Here the crowd are being entertained by a gentleman who played a violin accompanied on the piano by a young lady. Everyone, but the dog, who looks singularly unimpressed, appears to be enjoying the performance. In 1910 the remaining part of the Pier was removed leaving only the castle like entrance gate.

Opposite above: The Pier Towers in 1914. The wall then bore the nameboard, Central Promenade. On the right the sea spray can be seen as the seawall takes yet another pounding.

Opposite below: The Boating Lake, once a feature of the Promenade which runs alongside the Pier Towers. A boat ride was the high spot of a visit to the Promenade. This was the place where youngsters and dads came into their own, often waving to mums at the side of the lake.

The Old Pier Towers, Withernsea

An example of the tide battering the Promenade at Withernsea in the 1930s. There are very similar photographs spanning the decades; the town defences are under constant attack caused by the equinoxal tides which cause problems with erosion along the east coast. Recent abnormal tides have caused extensive damage to the wall, and work is now being carried out to strengthen these vital defences.

Opposite above: A later photograph of the Central Promenade taken in the 1950s showing a little more sophistication. The Ferris Wheel is well filled, and the parked cars indicate the visitors were now using private as well as public transport. The advertising board is offering trips to Bridlington and Scarborough.

Opposite below: This is a later view of Queens Parade with the Pier Towers in the distance. This postcard was published by a local firm in 1942, the summer of the air raid on the town.

Mr Cheverton Brown had a boat house at the bottom of his garden, which is roughly where the present Teddy's Club is now situated. He is said to have had a tunnel running from his house to the boat-house for easy access. During the storm of 1914, which severely damaged the promenade, the boat-house was badly affected, so he devised a plan for sea defences.

The year is 1914 and the Southcliffe Road Promenade was being built, but due to severely high tides, damage was done to the partly completed structure.

Two of the many patient donkeys who give rides on the sands, and pleasure to many youngsters during the season. Taken in 1911, no doubt some of the hatted ladies look fondly at their offspring in the saddle.

This donkey was snapped on Withernsea beach in the early 1920s, note the special saddle which nicely accommodates the small passengers. It is also interesting to see a group of horses waiting to attract riders for a trip along the sands.

THE SANDS, SOUTH CLIFF, WITHERNSEA.

The Beach. Withernsea

[V (4331)]

Beach, Withernsea.
Lister's Series. 1702

These are the wooden steps leading down to the beach at the end of Young Street. Catlin's Pierrots are performing to a large audience, whilst others are more attracted to the sea wall.

Opposite above: The beach at the south side of Withernsea was used by those who desired a quiet sojourn at the seaside. There were no amusements to disturb the peace. This was a space in which one could relax and if desired make sandcastles without fear of them being demolished by careless feet in a crowd. This beach was much used by people who stayed in the boarding houses in the streets that ran off from Queen Street to the Promenade.

Opposite below: A rather different view of the beach taken in 1914 with the fishermens boats very much in evidence. There are a few people watching the fishermen at work but this area is by no means as crowded as the more popular Pier Towers and North Promenade area.

The ubiquitous donkeys waiting patiently at the end of Seaside Road before starting their day on the beach in 1907. Until fairly recently (prohibitive regulations and heavy insurance coverage) no seaside town was complete without its beach donkeys. To generations of children a ride was an eagerly awaited treat, and to be allowed by the donkey man or lady to feed them with tit bits, such as a sugar lump, carrot or chopped apple, was an added bonus. Sadly, Withernsea, like many other resorts no longer have donkeys on their beaches.

An interesting photograph from the 1920s when Grapho's Jovial Jollies were at the height of their popularity in Withernsea. The alfresco Arcadia has been set up near the end of Seaside Road and shows some of the fishermen's boats in the foreground.

A happy little family group who surprisingly seem to have Withernsea beach to themselves. In view of the message on the back of the postcard the month was August and the year 1929, and the family name was Suddaby, from Hull.

'Oh, we do like to be beside the seaside!' Every resort had its 'Snaps' or the equivalent, and Withernsea was no exception. A man with a camera would tour the beaches and town taking photographs of groups and individuals. Next day prints were displayed at a central point, where for a modest fee, copies could be purchased by the holidaymakers to take home with them as a unique souvenir of their visit. A typical group was snapped on the beach at Withernsea in the 1920s.

522

Above: In the 1950s, during the holiday season, Withernsea had its own Beach Patrol. The young men were all volunteers who gave freely of their time to ensure the safety of the holidaymakers. The three lifeguards seated on the edge of the patrol boat are Peter Wright, Tony Siddle and Chuck Hunter.

Opposite above: A family group taken by Withernsea Snaps on the Promenade in August 1931. Note how the cameraman has obliterated the people in the background, thus highlighting his subject.

Opposite below: Enjoying the sun and sea, a happy mixed group of holidaymakers around 1930 pause for the camera. Note the bathing dresses, even the men are well covered, no swimming trunks.

THE SANDS, WITHERNSEA. 343-4.

WITHERNSEA, THE BEACH.

49753

This is obviously a group of ladies and gentlemen on an organised outing. The souvenir stall on the beach is interesting, on sale among other items are walking sticks. One feels that the two small urchins in the foreground are locals, rather than part of this formal looking.

Opposite above: Standing amid this animated beach scene is the stage of the Night Lights, a troupe of pierrots. They gave three shows a day at 11.00 am. and 7.30 pm. This was one of the few shows where seats could be booked in advance for the evening show which was given in the Co-op Hall. Shaw's swings can be seen in use, whilst many others are simply enjoying a peaceful sojourn on the beach.

Opposite below: Here we have the Night Lights again, this time the show is in full swing. Sadly for the performers the audience are mainly enjoying the show for free, although a few seats were occupied for this 1921 performance. The roundabouts and swings appear to be doing a good trade. These were owned by the Shaw family, who for generations operated the rides and at one time also ran the donkey concession on the beach. Fred Shaw eventually built his first amusement arcade on the site of the old donkey yard on Memorial Avenue.

A typical seaside outing which was an occasion eagerly anticipated by the participants. Above are children of varying ages, obviously in their 'best clothes'. Although some are possibly from poorer families an effort has been made by all. Here we have the Hull and District Band of Hope, apparently a group conducted by Mr. Frank H. Jefferson. There was always picnic food on such outings provided by the ladies committees, and many children enjoyed tasty morsels beyond their usual daily fare.

Three

The Pleasures of the Resort

In 1910 when the remaining part of the Pier was demolished, leaving just the Towers, the Council built a sea wall and Central Promenade with ornamental gardens. Here we see Mr. Cheverton Brown performing the opening ceremony at the new gardens.

The above photograph is of two gardeners at the Memorial Gardens in the 1920s. The man on the left was the resident gardener Fred Savage who was a qualified gardener. On the right is Len Walker who was his apprentice. Born in 1912 of an old Withernsea family, Len was to become a popular figure in the town. He spent some time working at the skating rink where he gave lessons for 6d. (2½p) per hour. In 1929 Len embarked on a marathon skating session which lasted for 73 hours and 20 minutes. This was a wooden rink adjoining the station. He joined the Volunteer Reserves, and was called up in 1939, serving seven years in the RAF. He is probably best remembered in the town for his work at Lee Avenue Swimming Pool where Len acted as instructor, being the holder of bronze and silver life saving medals, and the Lifeguard Medal which he won in 1934. Len's philosophy was always live and let live, and his recent death has left a gap in the community.

Lee Avenue Swimming Pool where Len worked was opened in 1911. It was built by Mr. Vickers Walker, a wealthy shipping owner, and was leased by him to the town council for a nominal rent with the understanding that it should be used only as a swimming pool. Originally it was filled with sea water which changed with every tide, but this was eventually replaced with fresh water. The swimming pool which gave joy to many children and adults alike has now gone.

An interesting view of the Italian Gardens and tennis courts taken in the 1920s. The town had a tennis club as early as 1901, but it was around 1911 that public tennis courts were provided. The path to the right is still in use leading from the Promenade to the Public Library and ultimately to south Queen Street. This was originally the garden belonging to Mr. Martin Cheverton Brown's house on Queen's Terrace that was bought for the council in 1922.

The once pleasant gardens along South Promenade are sadly no more. What was once a colourful amenity is now the site of a sewage plant and a boatyard for the local fishermen. The only remaining gardens are the Italian Gardens behind the Municipal Offices which are still well tended and pleasantly laid out. This postcard is one of a series produced by Wilf Lunn, who was not only the owner and editor of the local newspaper, but also a photographer and business man.

The Council Bowling Greens were officially opened on 27 April 1929. There was a very good turnout for the ceremony including bowlers and the general public. The official party included Mr. Chas Teall, the President of the Bowling Club, Councillor Wolverson, Mr. Ratcliffe, the Surveyor and Ex-Superintendent Sweeney.

This view of the Bowling Greens gives some idea of the Central Promenade area. There are signs saying that rock may be purchased also cigarettes. To the extreme left with the sign of the fish is Reg Redfern's Fish Shop. In the 1930s as a protest against the Shops Sunday Trading Act, Reg imported an automatic heated vending machine which was said to be the first of its kind in the country. Play is in progress on the bowling green, around which seats were placed for the convenience of spectators.

The Withernsea Ladies Hockey Club for the season 1907-08. Sport in the early part of the twentieth century was an integral part of life in Withernsea. By 1901 there were cricket and tennis clubs, the golf course opened in 1909. There are records of fairly regular athletic meetings, with some very desirable prizes for the winners. No doubt this group of ladies was considered quite daring by their older contemporaries.

Members of the 1908 Withernsea Ladies Cricket Team. According to contemporary newspaper reports they appear to have had a good season. It is daunting to think of a team of ladies taking to the field in the restrictive costumes of the day, but sport for ladies was beginning to be recognised and there were many successful teams throughout the country.

Four

Earning a Living

Connor and Graham's Buses were an institution around Withernsea and district. The company was started by two unemployed Geordies from South Shields who had been told by relatives that there was no public transport in this area. Shipyard workers James H. Graham and his brother-in-law Campbell (Con) Connor who were victims of the post-war depression came to Easington in 1921. They bought a fourteen seat Model T Ford bus for £250, which made its first journey to Hull on 21 October 1921. Soon they were prospering and purchased another bus. It is interesting to note that these buses were used in the TV production of Winifred Holtby's rural masterpiece *South Riding* which was filmed in Holderness. In 1954 Connor had turned to farming and was bought out by the Graham family. The company celebrated seventy years in business in 1991, but by 1994 had been taken over by the East Yorkshire Motor Services. Above shows one of their early buses leaving Spurn for Easington.

An interesting photograph of Withernsea Firemen and engine, which was taken in the 1920s. On the left is Fireman Saunders who served for thirty years. All of the town firefighters were volunteers who were employed in various different occupations, answering the call in emergencies. The current retained firemen in Withernsea still work under this principle.

A dramatic incident which took place a few decades ago on the Promenade near the Pier Towers. An overheated lorry caught fire which caused a mild sensation amongst holidaymakers who watched with interest as the local firemen tackled the blaze.

Holderness Gazette

With which is incorporated the "Withernsea Times," established 1910,
and the "Withernsea Gazette," established 1923.

Distributed in Withernsea, Patrington, Easington, Roos, Halsham and District.

Published Every Friday.

Women's Land Army

30,000
Recruits Required

A National Recruiting Campaign is being held during April. Write for particulars to the East Riding County Office, FINKLE STREET, YORK.

Food Comes First

The recent office-breaking into the premises of the Holderness Gas Company in Withernsea had a sequel at a special sitting of the magistrates on Monday, when three Hull youths were remanded in custody when charged with this offence, until April 18th.

The accused were Gordon Dickinson, aged 22 years, of St. Hilda Street, Hull, Leonard Ablitt, aged 19 years, of Beech Street, Hull, Leonard Pattinsor, aged 22 years, of Ella Street, Hull. Only evidence of arrest was given by Det. Con· Allison and P.C. Metcalf.

In 1910 Arthur Edward Lunn, a former journalist on the *Driffield Times* published his first edition of his own newspaper The *Withernsea Times*. It was a weekly free newspaper which was distributed throughout the town. In 1923 it became the *Withernsea Gazette*, Arthur Lunn set up his printing works in Walter Street, later moving to Seaside Road. Arthur died in 1934 and his youngest son John (Wilf) Lunn took over the newspaper along with his other business interests. Wilf was only 21, but under his direction the paper prospered and he became a well known figure in the town. It was a somewhat unique and interesting newspaper, Wilf having stamped his personality on it, and he reported in a style which was appealing and very much his own. During the Second World War and due to the fact that Wilf and most of his staff were serving in the armed forces, the paper was suspended, but his wife Elma, took over the running of the printing works. In 1946 he began to publish the newspaper again which he now called the *Holderness Gazette*, and continued to do so until he retired in 1980. Wilf was educated at Withernsea School, a truly local lad made good. He had many friends in the town and it was said he was always ready with a helping hand. Wilf was a business man and had other interests, but it is for the newspaper that he is mainly remembered. One person christened him by saying, 'Wilf was Mr. Withernsea'. Some of the postcards in this book were published by him, a fitting tribute to a man who loved the town. Pictured is Wilf on the right with his wife Elma, second left, enjoying a social occasion at the opening of a chalet park in Withernsea.

Expansion of Withernsea provided much needed work for local artisans. Here a group of builders are thought to be working at the end of Seaside Road in the vicinity of the Valley Gardens.

In the 1850s a member of the East Riding Constabulary was based in Withernsea, and a Police Station was built in Railway Crescent in 1891. In 1889 there was a police sergeant living in the town and a house was built for him at the Police Station in 1897. A Court House was built in 1898 where eventually the South Holderness Petty Sessions were held. The station itself was enlarged in 1905, and again when the new court was built in 1938. This group of policemen was photographed outside the Withernsea Police Station in 1929.

Five

Days of Learning

In 1870 W.E. Forster's Elementary Education Act instituted state provided and state maintained elementary schools. In areas where schools could not provide enough places for children, new schools were to be built from public funds. The first such in the area was the Owthorne Board School built in 1878. The first headmaster was Mr. Joseph Sissons who was at that time schoolmaster at the village of Airmyn near Goole. His salary was £80 per annum, and he remained with the school until his retirement in 1913. He died of pneumonia in 1921. The school was later known as Withernsea Council School.

Above: By 1921 Withernsea School, in spite of various additions of extra classrooms, was grossly overcrowded. A situation which would not be tolerated in these more enlightened times was that two classes were simultaneously being taught in the School Hall, one at each end. To ease this situation plans for a new building had been passed, and in 1921 it was opened. The 'New' building consisted of two ex-army wooden huts with an open veranda on the eastern side, and a gap was made in the playground. Locals remember these wooden huts as being very draughty and extremely cold. The young lady second from the left on the middle row, tells of grass growing up between the floor boards.

Above: A Christmas Fancy Dress Party at Miss A. Sherwood Shaw's St. Hubert's School of Music. The young man at the centre back is Walt Saunders, already at an early age playing the clown!

Right: An announcement of examination results of the St. Hubert's School of Music which appeared in the *Withernsea Gazette* in January 1929. The academy was held in very high esteem locally, and parents in some cases made very great efforts to find the few pennies to pay the modest fees for the dancing classes for their children.

Opposite below: Withernsea High School has long had a good sporting tradition. Seated in the centre is Headmaster Matthew Holmes. He was the first Headmaster of the new school, and held the post from 1935 to 1956, when in July of that year he reluctantly retired. The town was very fortunate to have the services of a man of the calibre of Matthew Holmes, who, with great foresight, built a good foundation for the new school. An annual holiday was kept, paying tribute to his inspired leadership. This is the Withernsea High School Second XI of 1953-54. Back row, left to right: D. Starkey, B. Greensides, D. Beadle, T. Robinson, P. Wright. Seated: J. Metcalfe, J. Ingamells, Captain. Mr Holmes, J. Crane, Vice Captain and J. Parry. Front: B. Lawton and R. Wigglesworth.

ST. HUBERT'S SCHOOL OF MUSIC

PRINCIPAL

Miss A. Sherwood Shaw.

All Lessons resumed Jan. 16th.

DANCING:

Adults' Class : Thursday, Jan. 17th, at 8-0 p.m.

Children's Class : Sat. Morn., Jan. 19th at 10-30.

At the recent examination of The Associated Board of the Royal Academy and Royal College of Music, the following candidates were successful. Piano—Higher Division, Kathleen Kirk ; Primary, Ena Woodhouse. Violin—Higher Division, John Ashwell (Honourable Mention). London College of Music : Elocution—Winifred Gardner (Diploma) ; Elementary, Joyce Stott and Elain Stott.

St. Hubert's House was originally built as a summer residence for Lucy Ann Soulby who was the Lady of the Manor at East Keal near Spilsby in Lincolnshire. Each year Lucy, who was a widow, came to Withernsea which was at that time a very fashionable place. With her came her married daughter and grandchildren, also domestic staff to provide for their comfort. At a later period it was owned by Peter Robson of Moore & Robson's Brewery. When the photograph was taken the house was run by two ladies, Miss Shaw and Miss Rhodes, who taught dancing and the piano. It was then called St. Huberts School of Music, and is reputed to have boasted an excellent dance floor. It is now the business premises of a local accountant. There are stories which suggest that the house may be haunted, but there is no evidence to substantiate the stories.

Six

Guarding Our Coast

During the sixteenth century there were three beacons in Withernsea, this being a way of warning shipping. The first lifeboat station was established in 1862 with a boat house in Arthur Street. The boathouse in Seaside Road was built in 1881-82 and used until 1913. The Arthur Street building housed the life saving rocket apparatus. The Coastguard Station was built in 1905 on Marine Parade, and was in use until 1951 when it was decided that it was no longer necessary to keep a full watch at Withernsea.

On Christmas Day 1904 the trawler *Leonora of Grimsby* was stranded on the beach at Waxholme. This postcard which was sent to Miss Sallie Woodhouse at the Post Office, Withernsea, tells her that on the 18 February 1905, the ship was still grounded and could not be refloated.

Opposite above: The life-jacketed crew climb aboard the *Admiral Rous* Lifeboat preparatory to a launching at Withernsea. The first Admiral Rous Lifeboat was provided from a bequest left by the late Henry John Rous in 1877. His legacy provided two lifeboats, the *Admiral Rous* and the *Admiral Rous II*, and also in 1882, a new boathouse. He joined the navy in 1808 and rose through the ranks, retiring in 1866 as an Admiral.

Opposite below: On the occasions when the Withernsea lifeboat had to be launched it was drawn to the beach on a carriage by horses, the number of horses seems to have varied no doubt through availability. Once in the sea, the boat was released from the carriage with the crew on board, the horses being used to give the lifeboat momentum. Here, after the successful launch, the carriage is being drawn ashore manually.

LAUNCHING THE WITHERNSEA LIFEBOAT

Launch of the Lifeboat, Withernsea

Spurn is unusual in respect of the community having a full time lifeboat crew. This photograph taken in 1909 shows the coastguard station. It was taken over by the Royal National Lifeboat Institution in 1913.

Spurn is the peninsula which is bordered by the North Sea on one side and the Humber Estuary on the other. It has a history of erosion and has on occasion been breached. From as far back as the middle ages it has been considered a menace to shipping, and has had several lighthouses of varying efficiency. The one presently standing was built in 1852. This view taken from the north west is of the tip of the peninsula and clearly shows the position of the lighthouse, also the lifeboatmen's houses. It was taken just after the turn of the twwntieth century.

A view of the lighthouse taken from Arthur Street. This was one of the streets on the first plan for building in Withernsea along with the Esplanade (Bannister Street), Young Street, Walter Street and Edward Street. Edward Street can be discerned in this 1932 view to the left, it still remains but is more or less a very wide alleyway.

Withernsea in the latter part of the nineteenth century had a sad record of sea disasters. A particularly significant disaster was the grounding of the Grimsby fishing vessel *Genista* on 18 October 1890. At the subsequent inquest the Coroner opined that the tragedy may have been avoided if the town had possessed a lighthouse. Trinity House decided that one should be erected, and between 1892-93, over a period of eighteen months it was built, thus reducing the number of wrecks in the area quite dramatically. The lighthouse is octagonal in shape and built of brick and concrete. It is 120 feet high and is topped by a gigantic weathervane in the shape of an arrow, which was connected to a compass on the inside of the roof to enable the keeper to check wind direction. The light was 113 feet above the ground and reached by a spiral staircase of some 144 steps. The first two keepers were Mr. Ross and Mr. Robbins who lived in the house and cottage attached. The light first shone on the 1 March 1894. The light was last seen on the 1 July 1976, a span of 82 years. Another claim to fame is that it was said to be the only lighthouse in the country with a town between it and the sea. It is now the town museum.

THE LIGHTHOUSE, WITHERNSEA

Mrs. Quinton of Easington who is sending her picture to her son who was stationed at the Coastguard Station at Bray, County Wicklow, Ireland in 1907.

Mr. Quinton of Easington whose picture was sent by his wife in 1907 to another son who was also a coastguard at Station Winterton near Yarmouth. She tells him there is no fresh news of the family.

Withernsea lifeboat the *Docea Chapman* taking part in the Coronation Parade for George V in 1911. The boat is being drawn down Princess Avenue and is about to turn into King Street. Coxwain Robert Drewery rides in the boat, the man in the peaked cap at the front. The *Docea Chapman* was built by the Thomas Ironworks. She was a self righting Rubie Class boat which cost £830. She was the last of the Withernsea offshore lifeboats and was bought from a legacy left by Mr. Joseph Chapman in memory of his late wife.

Sacred to the Memory

of

GEORGE KETTLE,
AGED 41 YEARS,
GEORGE FITCH,
AGED 21 YEARS,
WILLIAM GANT,
AGED 18 YEARS,
ALSO JAMES JOHN LAMB,
AGED 33 YEARS,
WHO IS INTERRED AT HOLMPTON,
NATIVES OF COLCHESTER, WHO WERE
DROWNED IN THE STORM OF OCTr
23rd 1880.

During the great storm of 23 October 1880, the pier, like many others on
the North East coast was severely damaged. This gravestone in St. Nicholas
Churchyard was erected to the memory of George Kettle aged 41, George Fitch
aged 21, William Gant aged 18 and James Lamb aged 33, who it was stated was
interred at Holmpton. These men were drowned when their boat collided with
the pier, damaging a large part of the structure. After several such incidents over
the next three decades, only the ornamental castellated gate remained in 1910,
the last remaining portion having been removed.

Seven

The Church in the Community

OPENING NEW PARISH ROOMS WITHERNSEA 6.5.14
PHOTO
C CARTONE STUDIOS   Nº 2

The Church Institute was built in 1913-14 adjoining the graveyard. The Vicar of St. Nicholas in 1914 when the new Parish Rooms were opened was the Reverend J.F. Tomlinson. The foundation stone for the building was laid by the wife of the Rural Dean, the Reverend N.J. Miller of Winestead.

St. Nicholas Parish Church, Withernsea.

After the village of Withernsea was taken by the sea, a new church was consecrated at a place which was further inland called Priest Hill in 1448. This suffered severely from the elements, at one period having the roof torn off. It was restored and refurbished in 1858-59 and is now the present church of St. Nicholas. From the late eighteenth century it is thought that there were probably two services each Sunday, and Holy Communion was celebrated six times a year. This was gradually increased, becoming fortnightly, and finally each senite. The cost of restoration was met by public subscription and a very generous donation made by the Hull and Holderness Railway Company.

The church has a chancel and clerestoried nave with a south porch and west tower. The chancel is of ashlar, and is, with many churches in Holderness, built with cobbles and boulders. In 1894 the church had seven bells made by James Barnwell of Birmingham.

A rare view of St. Nicholas' Church, with the Church House centre, and the Convalescent Home to the right of the photograph.

A happy occasion when on 12 July 1901 a Garden party was held at the St. Matthew's Vicarage. The church has always provided social events for its congregation, such as concerts, bazaars, garden parties and the like. In Withernsea there were plenty of activities of this nature promoted by all church denominations.

The Wesleyan Methodist Chapel in North Gate in the parish of Owthorne was registered in 1804. It was later replaced by a chapel in Cammidge Street built in 1857.

At the north end of Withernsea a chapel of ease was built on Waxholme Road by Elizabeth Swann. This was a brick building and is thought to have been built by the father of George Cammidge. In 1857 it was licensed for worship and dedicated to St. Matthew. It was restored in 1883 and a chancel added in 1890. The chapel was replaced by a new church in Hull Road in 1935, and was then used as a church hall. It was demolished in 1971. In the early days there was one service on Sundays, but this was increased to two and occasionally three. Holy Communion being held monthly.

On 24 July 1879 the Primitive Methodist Chapel on Hull Road came into use. There does not appear to have been any official opening, but a series of special services were held throughout July, August and September of that year. The Reverend G. Lamb of Hull preached there at 3.00 pm and 7.00 pm.

A fine picture of the Wesleyan Chapel built in 1900-01. It was built by the Primitive's Chapel Steward W.H. Carr. A schoolroom was later added in 1907. The cost of the building was £3,000, and the seating capacity was for 450. The building to the left of the chapel tower, standing on the corner of Young Street is the bakery and shop once owned by the Watts family. They were highly regarded in the town and area for their high quality baking. This link was broken only a few years ago when the two elderly sisters who ran the business finally retired.

HOLDERNESS CHAMBERS MISSION HALL,
Queen Street, Withernsea.

GREAT REVIVAL CAMPAIGN

in the above Hall, will be conducted by

Evangelist Rawson [Rotherham]

Commencing Saturday, Dec. 3rd, at 3 p.m., to Dec. 18th,
inclusive at 7·30 each evening (except Friday) Sundays 3 and 6·30 p.m.

Saturday, December 3rd, at 3 p.m.

A Special Programme by the Lee Smith Street Mission
String Band and Choir
along with a short address by Mr. Smith.
6 p.m. Procession through Town,
7 p.m. Special Gospel Service
Speaker—Evangelist Astwood, Rotherham

Also PERCY CALLADINE (ex-Middle-weight Champion of Yorkshire
and Midlands) will give an up-to-date testimony of his conversion on a
racecourse.

Sunday, December 4th, at 7·30 p.m.

A SPECIAL SERVICE in the Kinema Picture House
(kindly loaned to us)
when the above speakers will be present.

Admission Free.   Hymn Sheets Provided.   Everybody Welcome.

No connection with any work in Withernsea, or who has been in
Withernsea—entirely a new Mission Work.

Not only were there Anglican, Protestant and a Catholic Church in the town, but also Quakers, Christian Scientists and by 1946 Jehovah's Witnesses. This advertisement from the *Withernsea Gazette* tells of a Revival Campaign in 1938. The meeting was led by Evangelist Rawson of Rotherham and included all the attractions of this kind of venture. It was the usual practice to present to those assembled a 'converted sinner' to give testimony, in this instance an ex-champion boxer.

St. Matthew's Church Choir pictured in 1924 during the Easter services. The Vicar is the Reverend W. Leonard, seated between Mr and Mrs G. Land. the young man on the extreme left of the front row is Wilf Lunn, who was to become a very well known figure in the town.

Eight

That's Entertainment

The Floral Hall was built by the Council in 1922 on Pier Road. It could seat around 700 people, and was often filled to capacity during the summer season. Shows of all kinds were staged in the Floral Hall including pierrots, concerts, and almost anything with entertainment value. Prices for admittance were very reasonable. In 1937 admission was 1s. (5p), 9d. (3½p), 6d. (2½p), children half price. When the pavilion was built in 1938 the Floral Hall closed and was demolished. The war memorial to the left, which records those who gave their lives in the First World War, was later moved to the Italian Gardens.

A happy occasion at the Grand Pavilion which was opened in 1938, a childrens Christmas party just before the outbreak of war. The Master of Ceremonies on the left is Wal Clinton, a seasoned performer both on stage and concert party platform. Wal was well known in Withernsea as an Entertainment Manager. He first came to the old Rink and later took over the management of the Grand Pavilion. He left Withernsea shortly after the outbreak of hostilities, and sadly died in Leeds in 1944. The clown on the tricycle is a local personality, Walt Saunders, who for many years played the clown in the annual carnival procession. He was a signwriter and decorator by trade, one of his regular jobs was supplying the film posters for the local cinema.

Opposite: Walt Saunders in his clown suit, a man who brought happiness to so many people. By trade a signwriter and decorator, he was a true entertainer. In its early years, no Withernsea Carnival Parade would be complete without Walt. He was born in 1906 and died in 1974, and after cremation, his ashes were scattered on the sea near the PierTowers. A saying popular with some of his old friends if any argument arose which needed arbitration was 'Ask him down there', whilst pointing at the sea, meaning Walt will know.

Unity Hall, the scene of many entertainments of all kinds in Withernsea was part of the Co-op premises on the corner of Pier Road and Queen Street. It was opened in 1915. This group of young people who called themselves 'The Twenty Club' met at the hall regularly for social events. The group are attending a dance held in the hall on the 28th of October 1927.

The cast of the Mikado on stage at the Floral Hall. This was a local Operatic Society production, one of many in the 1920s and 1930s. A Gilbert and Sullivan production was an annual event, which was eagerly awaited by a faithful audience.

A rather different group of entertainers who appeared in Withernsea in 1912 were Joe Ellison's Entertainers. Instead of the traditional pom-poms and ruffles, their image was that of well-dressed young men about town, complete with smart blazers and straw boater hats. The style of entertainment was still family oriented, and they were basically beach performers.

Regular visitors to the resort, Tadman's Unique's Concert Party performed on Withernsea beach. Famous comedian Bunny Doyle made what might be termed his earliest appearance on stage, when in 1908, whilst on holiday at Withernsea, he entered a Talent Contest organised by Tadman. Another famous comedian, Hull born Dick Henderson (senior) also made his first appearances on Withernsea Beach with pierrots. He later, like his son Dickie Henderson, achieved great fame both on stage and screen in Britain and America.

Here we have the local orchestra on stage at the Unity Hall. The names of operettas performed by the local Gilbert and Sullivan players appear behind them. The saxophonist, second from the left, next to the standing man, is Herman Baker, and the lady between the drummer and pianist is Lotte Baker, the father and mother of the famous jazz trumpeter Kenny Baker.

Opposite: The celebrated international trumpet player Kenny Baker was born at 73 Queen Street, Withernsea in 1921. He is now 74 years of age. His father and mother Herman and Lotte Baker were by profession shoemakers who came from Northamptonshire and set up business in Withernsea after the Great War. Both being very talented musicians, it was not surprising that at the tender age of 13 Kenny began playing the cornet in the local Gospel Mission Band. In the 1930s the family moved to Hull and young Kenny joined the West Hull Silver Prize Excelsior Band. In 1939 he went back to the Midlands, and in 1942 he joined the RAF and played with the famous wartime Squadronaires. He has over the years worked with many famous bands, Ambrose, Jack Jackson, Lew Stone, Geraldo and Jack Hylton to name but a few. In 1949 he formed his own band and his career rocketed. Kenny played solo trumpet in the film Genevieve with Withernsea actress Kay Kendall, miming for the cameras. After almost sixty years as a professional trumpeter Kenny is still playing, and his 'Baker's Dozen' are still extremely popular with both musicians and music fans alike.

Left: Will Catlin the 'King of the Pierrots' chose Charles Milner to manage his Withernsea troupe. Milner was very versatile being a character comedian, pianist and singer. He married Jenny Arnott, whose brother Chas was also a Catlin man. He is seen here surrounded by his 'boys' in 1905. The season ran from March to September. The performers varied over the years and some moved on to other troupes and new members were added. The 'boys' stayed every year with a lady who ran a boarding house on Queen Street. Pierrots were always a popular form of entertainment at the seaside. Their shows were always family orientated, the performers were versatile, and the programmes varied. The entertainment was not costly, and could even be free if one was mean enough to avoid the 'bottler' when he came round the crowd with his collecting bag.

Below: In 1909, Ernie Preston, a local boy, joined the popular Catlin's Pierrots under the management of Charles Milner. He was a well liked member, both by his colleagues and the local audiences, who went along to 'give our Ernie a good clap'. He died in a London hospital in 1959.

Opposite above: Several pierrot troupes appeared at Withernsea over the years, but none was more popular than Bert Grapho's Jovial Jollies, who during the day appeared on the beach, and in the evenings in the Floral Hall. Popular throughout the twenties, they were booked to appear as usual for the 1929 season, when the sad news came that on 11 May, Bert Grapho had died. He was highly respected in the town and many people were saddened by his passing. When it became known that his widow with the help of their son Jack, had decided that the show must go on, the townsfolk really took the company to their hearts. It is recorded that many acts of kindness were shown to Mrs Grapho in tribute to her courage and showmanship.

Right: This advertisement is from the local newspaper in 1929. There is an accompanying report which indicates that the show played to full houses. Bert's son Jack, led the show. The two artistes mentioned were very popular, Tony Spoors played the piano, and it was said that he 'was able to play anything at all'. The rotund La Tagarte popularly known as 'Larty Garty' whose full name was William Tagarte Craugon, claimed to have sung at the La Scala Opera House in Milan, and had a fine baritone voice.

FLORAL HALL,

Lessee : E. Grapho.   Manager : Sid Vance.

—

BERT GRAPHO'S

" JOVIAL "
JOLLIES

"The Old Firm."

—

Thursday Night, September 5th,

BENEFIT

TO

LA TAGARTE

AND

TONY SPOORS.

Book your seats at Nicholson's Music Shop.

These popular entertainers are appearing at the Floral Hall in 1922. Many pierrots like Horace West performed primarily on the beach but gave evening performances at an indoor venue.

Opposite: Irene Lawson was born in Hull, and was taught to dance as a child by Madame Sharrah, who enjoyed a very high reputation, with several of her pupils becoming famous. In the early 1930s, Irene, who was then working for the Hull firm of confectioners, Needlers, moved to Withernsea where her mother kept a boarding house. In 1933 at the age of seventeen, Irene began teaching dancing in the town, whilst still commuting to Hull via the six o'clock morning train. When she opened her dancing school, Irene adapted the name of her late employers, naming her enterprise The Reldene School of Dancing, which Irene Lawson, BEM, still runs to this day, being one of the most highly respected personalities in Withernsea.

Always a popular event eagerly awaited in Withernsea, the Crowning of the Rose Queen in the grounds of the Convalescent Home. This usually took place in August to coincide with Carnival Week, and many regular visitors arranged their holidays specially to include these dates.

Opposite above: Dominated by the lighthouse, the premises on the corner of Hull Road where Irene and her husband were to set up home, and found her dance class in later years.

Opposite below: Every year since that date, Irene has produced a pantomime and the Rose Queen Festival in the town. There were also other concerts and productions too numerous to mention, and all of the money raised over the years has been donated to various charities, including wartime comforts funds and the Red Cross. Irene became Mrs Sindall and she and her husband lived on the upper floor of the shop seen on the left of the picture, here she used the lower floor for her dance classes. For purely professional reasons she retained the name Lawson. Here we see the pupils on Hull Road about to turn right into Queen Street with the Rose Queen procession of 1954.

Irene with two pupils as she celebrated 40 years of shows in the town. The venues were varied including the Floral Hall, where she staged her first show, Unity Hall, the Grand Pavilion and the Church Institute to name but a few. During the war years the children often had to wear paper dresses, but nothing deterred Irene. She has now celebrated 60 years of shows and has no intentions of giving up dancing. In 1992, Irene was awarded the BEM for her long service to the community, having now given several thousands of pounds to charity. She met HRH Prince Charles on his recent visit to Withernsea, he echoed the sentiments of her many friends 'Well done, keep up the good work'.

A young lady called Justine McCarthy was born in Withernsea in 1926. She was the daughter of Terry McCarthy, who with his sister Pat were a dance team who played under the stage name of Kendall. This was no doubt from their famous grandmother Marie Kendall who was a great Music Hall artist. When young Justine began to make her way as an actress, she became Kay Kendall. She had a brother Terry and a sister Kim, their grandfather was a well known Withernsea character Robert Drewery. Here Kay is seen in what is perhaps her best remembered film Genevieve (1953) miming a trumpet solo, which ironically was actually played by the famous Withernsea born jazz musician Kenny Baker. Kay, contracted leukemia and died in 1959 at the tragically young age of 32.

After the Second World War, in spite of the attempts to revive pierrot shows, like other resorts Withernsea had little success. One such troupe who did at least achieve local acclaim were the Hollym Follies who began in 1962 under the direction of Florence Coverdale. The group consisted of seven dancers, Mary Talbot, Mary Carmichael, June Smith, Ena Stephenson, Clarice Briggs, Doreen Dennis and Doris Ledger. They were all members of the Womens Institute, and their first amateur show was such a success they decided to continue entertaining people both in Withernsea and around the villages. They continued to do so until they disbanded in 1979-80.

Withernsea was the place chosen by the Mexborough heavyweight boxer William 'Iron' Hague (1885-1951) as the venue to prepare for his fight with the formidable black American boxer Sam Langford. Hague, who was the new British Champion, having defeated Gunner Moir on 22 May 1909, lodged with his retinue at the Pier Hotel. The adjoining Assembly Rooms were fitted out for Hague as an indoor training headquarters. Punch bags and other apparatus was set up, as well as provision for an indoor running track for use in wet weather. When asked about Withernsea, Hague replied laconically, 'Oh its a grand place, for an invalid! Its a place where you want your dinner two hours before its ready'. The special representative of the Mexborough and Swinton Times related back to his readers, 15 May 1909. 'Hague continues to be an object of interest and admiration, and some speculation. There are foolish people in the district who have not yet realised that Hague is the most powerful heavyweight in the world, and at Barnsley and Rotherham odds are being quoted at 5 to 4 against. Langford's reputation must indeed be great. Motor-bus excursions to Withernsea have been arranged in order to give Mexboro' people an opportunity of seeing the tail end of the training, when 'Iron' Hague is probably looking at his best, and the railway excursions will also be patronised'. The manager of the National Sporting Club Mr. A.F. Bettinson journeyed to Withernsea on the 21 May to inform the boxer that the fight would be for the Championship of the World as Langford was regarded by many as the legitimate champion. This was not true however as Jack Johnson was still recognised as the World Champion after defeating Tommy Burns in 1908, and successfully defending the title several times until he lost it to Jess Willard in 1915.

Sam Langford (c.1883-1956) or as he was affectionately known to boxing fans 'The Boston Tar Baby' was one of the greatest heavyweight boxers ever to have laced on the gloves. A small man for a heavyweight boxer, standing at five feet seven inches, he was as broad across the shoulders as he was tall, with a huge barrel chest and long muscular arms which carried a deadly punch in each fist. He had toppled all of the great names early twentieth century, including the legendary Jack Johnson, who had a healthy respect for his coloured compatriot. On his second trip to England in 1909, his manager Joe Woodman was persuaded to match his man with the new British Champion at the National Sporting Club in London. The new British Champion was Iron Hague who had just won the title from Gunner Moir. Though it soon became apparent that Hague was no match for the American, he knocked him over in the fourth round with a smashing blow to the left ear. So terrific was Hague's punch, the Tar Baby turned a complete catherine wheel in the ring. As he rose to his feet, Langford hit Hague with a solid right hook which knocked the Yorkshireman out for the full count. A real character, many anecdotes pepper the career of this boxing legend. Once, whilst fighting an opponent in America, with whom it has been agreed beforehand that Langford would take it easy and go for a points win, his opponent became bolder as Langford's punches carried no power. Thinking he could actually win, he set about Langford in no mean fashion. Langford soon realised what was happening, and at the bell commencing a round rang, he held out his hand as if to shake for the last round. His opponent pointed out that it was not the last round. 'It is foh you' Langford whispered in his ear, 'Ise waistin no moh time' then knocked him out with the one solid blow he threw during the fight.

The Pier Hotel on the corner of Bannister Street and Seaside Road was built in 1879. The Assembly Rooms were added in 1901, and burnt down in 1913. In the early part of the twentieth century Mr and Mrs Ramstar were mine hosts. The service was excellent and the amenities offered by the hotel were first class. The Assembly Rooms were a popular venue for a number of social activities. Charles Milner, manager of Catlin's Pierrots in the town staged shows there in addition to those on the beach. He and his family stayed at the hotel each season for fourteen years until he joined the armed forces in 1914. His daughter Marie, who spoke to us, the writers of this book, some years ago, remembered Mr and Mrs Ramstar for their kindness and consideration to others. The Assembly Rooms were also used for training purposes by the celebrated boxer Iron Hague when he was preparing for his fight with the black American boxer Sam Langford 'The Boston Tar baby' in 1909. The outward appearance of the hotel has changed little over the years, having recently been sympathetically restored.

Nine

The Parade Goes By

King Edward VII was a very popular figure in East Yorkshire, and when he died on 6 May 1910, he was greatly mourned. On the day of his funeral an enterprising Hull photographer, Robert Watson of Anlaby Road, filmed the funeral. This was rushed through and shown at the Assembly Rooms the same evening. Remembering this was well before the advent of television, and the rooms were packed. On 20 May 1910 a commemorative service was held in the church after a parade watched by soberly dressed onlookers.

PATRINGTON MAY FESTIVAL. 1914. Nº 17.

Above: The May Festival parade at Patrington in 1914, headed by the Queen and her two youthful male attendants. Some of the children in the parade are holding the traditional May garlands. The spectators appear to be accompanying the parade to its destination where the seasonal festivities would take place.

Right: The Patrington May Queen of 1913, with her attendants dutifully holding the train of her dress.

Opposite above: May Festival has always been celebrated in the Holderness area, with the inherent agonies of choosing the May Queen and her attendants. Then on the day there would be a parade culminating in the crowning of the Queen in some suitable place where there was usually a maypole erected for dancing around. This little group were participants in the 1913 festival in Withernsea.

Opposite below: Four very smartly turned out boys performing a song for the Withernsea May Festival of 1913. The title of the song was, appropriately 'The Tall Top Hat'.

The Coronation Parade seen here passing Mr. Cheverton Brown's house on Queen's Terrace. The parade included representatives of the lifeboat crews and other local services. There were floats, fancy dress and bands, and numerous other attractions for the edification of resident and visitor alike.

King George V was crowned on 22 June 1911, a little over a year after the demise of King Edward VII. Withernsea, like almost every other town and village in the realm celebrated this occasion. Strollers on the Promenade watch a band pass by, one of the many which took part in the magnificent parade.

A patriotic float with John Bull and Britannia supported by representatives of its army and navy with a bevy of pretty attendants. The costumed ladies represent some European countries and also India, possibly in celebration after the end of the Great War. The people of Withernsea were very supportive of their country and the promotion of peace.

A happy scene as Withernsea Carnival makes its way down Queen Street. The period being the early 1930s and as usual the parade is being led by local clown Walt Saunders on Dewey the donkey.

An ornately decorated car bound for the Carnival Parade in 1924 paused outside Scott's Watchmakers on Queen Street, much to the delight of the onlookers at the upstairs window. It is interesting to note that even the spoked wheels have been decorated with ribbons.

The Carnival King and Queen at the Pier Towers after being crowned. Photographs of the event were very quickly offered for sale as the message on the back of this postcard states 'Withernsea Wednesday' and relates that the picture shows the prizewinners on the previous Saturday.

WITHERNSEA CARNIVAL

P185

36.

This gives a good idea of the variety of carnival processions. There is a cart being heaved along manually by a man and a boy, there are horses, also a lovely little donkey cart followed by an East Yorkshire open topped bus and other motor traffic. Then as now, the streets were lined with people along the route which meanders through the town. There is still a great enthusiasm for the parade, and many people work very hard to produce imaginative and amusing floats.

Opposite above: A Photo Snaps picture of Withernsea Carnival in the late 1920s. A group of people in fancy dress are standing in front of one of the many highly decorated floats which were a main feature of the carnivals.

Opposite below: A happy group of all ages in fancy dress for the 1924 Carnival Parade. The photograph was taken in the gardens in front of the houses on North Promenade.

On a Sunday morning in September 1908, a man gave himself up to the police in Withernsea, admitting to murdering a woman the previous evening. His name was Charles Henry Woodman aged 22. His victim was Kate Lee, a 21 year old barmaid at the Queens Hotel. Woodman, of Hull, who had become infatuated with Kate visited her for the weekend, and became jealous when he saw her in the company of another man. He took her for a walk and then cut her throat. It was revealed at this trial at York Assizes that his father had spent twenty years in an asylum, and he was declared unfit to plead. Woodman was detained indefinitely, thus escaping the gallows. A vast crowd turned out for Kate Lee's funeral, one suspects that many came out of curiosity rather than respect.

The Murder Seat! This is the seat where Charles Henry Woodman allegedly took Kate Lee to talk to her before slitting her throat in 1908. Photographs of the seat proved popular though somewhat macabre souvenirs at the time.

Ten

Withernsea at War

This group of St. John's nurses with Dr. Young on the left and Dr. Fouracre on the right, were photographed in 1938. Were the sandbags part of the precautions being taken at that period when it was obvious to many people that war with Germany was inevitable?

Above: On 24 July 1942 the people of
Withernsea and the holidaymakers were
quietly going about their business when,
in the early evening the unthinkable
happened. One observer tells how she,
along with her mother and grandmother,
were walking along Queen Street when
their eyes were attracted upwards by an
aeroplane flying overhead. They, like other
people, took it for one of ours setting
out on a raid over Germany. Much to
everyones amazement it turned and they
were horrified to see bombs raining down.
The first landed on the Promenade, the
second on Queen Street. Two ladies and
a bus driver were killed and many were
injured. Casualties were taken to the
Municipal Buildings which were used
as a clearing station, some of the more
seriously wounded being transferred to
Beverley. The scene above shows the
devastation of the premises shown left.
There are reports that the following day
German Aircraft returned and machine
gunned along Queen Street, the main
thoroughfare. There does not appear to be
any record of casualties on this day.

Opposite below: This is Turner's Paint and Wallpaper Shop on Queen Street in 1936, sporting a jolly Father Christmas. The Turner family have a long tradition in the painting and decorating business. After the German raid in 1942, a new shop was built on the site and is still a family business today.

Above: Miss Eileen Saunders was Withernsea's first Bus Conductress. In May 1940 Eileen who was caring for her sick mother heard that E.Y.M.S. were seeking part time employees, and decided this was to be her war effort. Her shift on the first Monday morning began at 5.30 am and ended at 2.30 pm. After one week training she was given her own bus which was No. 3639. Eileen tells of her time on the buses as five years of very hard work, but also a time which she enjoyed and made many friends. She recalls experiences of German air raids on the journeys to and from Hull, and the many amusing anecdotes of some of her passengers.

Right: Withernsea Red Cross nurse Mary Walker sent this postcard to a friend 'With my best respects in 1939'. Both men and women in Withernsea were quick to answer the call to arms when hostilities broke out. Many served in varying capacities, along with those who for varying reasons found it more practical to offer their voluntary services to organisations like the A.R.P., Fire Service and St. John's Ambulance Brigade.

The photographs reproduced here were taken in the access entrance behind Bannister Street and the former Watt's Bakery premises. The partygoers include members of what have been called the old Withernsea families, including the Thompsons, Philips, Holmes, Youngs, Bowens, Downs and others.

VE Day (Victory in Europe) on 8 May 1945 was a day of celebration throughout Britain. Street parties were rapidly organised, wives and mothers produced amazing party food from meagre rations, there was music and dancing in the street. Even bulky pianos were manhandled outside to make sure the occasion went with a swing.

Eleven

Around and About

In May 1934, the celebrated writer Winifred Holtby stayed in Withernsea for several weeks gathering material for her novel *South Riding*. The town of Kiplington in the novel is based on Withernsea and the settlement known as the Shacks, was inspired by Holmpton Road Camp. This part of her story follows the fortunes of one Fred Mitchell, insurance agent and Barnabas Holly, builders labourer and their families. The novel was published in 1936 after her death in 1935, and is probably her finest work, winning the James Tait Black Memorial Prize in 1937. Many other local places thinly veneered in the story are easily recognisable to Holderness people. The photograph above showing part of Holmpton Road Camp was taken in 1911.

Halsham has always been a farming village, originally it was divided into East Halsham and West Halsham. The Constable family made their home in the village from the twelfth to the seventeenth century. The family mausoleum is still in the village although the house has gone. In 1597 they founded a Free School and Alms Hospital. At some time in the nineteenth century it became the school which is shown above, which could accommodate fifty children. The building still stands but is no longer a school, it is a private residence known as Halsham House.

RED HALL, WINSTEAD. 6497

From early times Winestead was the property of the Hildyard family. Around 1720 the Red Hall was built for the family, an earlier house having been demolished. It was so named for the obvious reason that it was built with red bricks. In 1932 the property was acquired by Hull Corporation. In 1936 the house was demolished to make way for a hospital. Andrew Marvell was born in the village in 1621. His reputation today is that of a poet, but he was also an assiduous Member of Parliament, of whom it was said 'was a thoroughly honest man in an age of corruption'.

A group of local entertainers, the Merry Milkmaids from Roos, appearing with what seems to be a wedding party complete with Vicar in August 1924.

Opposite above: Sunk Island is unique being land reclaimed from the sea. It is flanked by the River Humber, and has since its reclamation been a farming community. It is also the inspiration for Cold Harbour Colony in Winifred Holtby's novel *South Riding*. A resettlement scheme for men discharged from the forces after the Great War was set up by the Ministry of Agriculture and became Sunk Island Crown Colony. Sadly this was not a success, many of the men being from urban backgrounds and not suited to agricultural work. The gentleman on the horse is Mr. Oldfield with Mr. Downing inspecting the Strays where the cattle grazed.

Opposite below: This group were photographed in the mid 1920s. The occasion was the presentation of what appears to be a very handsome clock to Mr. Oldfield who was the first Bailiff of Sunk Island Crown Colony. Those present were members of the community who knew and worked with Mr. Oldfield.

One of the many garden parties held at Bleak House, Patrington, the home of Doctor Coates, who is seated alongside his wife in the centre of the front row. Born in 1869, he was a remarkable man, being a surgeon, barrister and county councillor to name but a few of his accomplishments. He was noted for the parties held at his home, many being for charitable causes, others for the Liberal party, being a great supporter. This gathering is particularly interesting as he was reputed to have owned one of the first motor cycles in the area, and many tales are still related of his exploits on his machine. He was undoubtedly one of the most respected and outstanding characters around south Holderness, and was greatly mourned when he died in 1924 aged 55.

Opposite above: There have been settlements in Holderness since the days of the Vikings and Roos is one such site. It has been associated through the ages with Drogo, and in later years with the Sykes of Sledmere. Robert Roos fought for Richard the Lionheart, and saw King John grant the Magna Carta. This peaceful scene with a mother and daughter enjoying the sunshine, and others who have paused in their work embodies the spirit of life in a rural community.

Opposite below: Early in the twentieth century, cycling became very popular, both for practicality and pleasure. Nellie and Emma are the two young ladies standing with their bicycles at Roos. Note the back wheels of their cycles have string guards to prevent their skirts becoming entangled in the wheels, and also another safety feature, the enclosed bicycle chains.

One of the earliest buildings in Patrington Market Place was a shop owned by St Patricks Church. In the latter part of the nineteenth century it was leased to Elizabeth Robinson whose business, so the sign above the door tells us, was established in 1870, as what we would now refer to as a high class drapery. It has been recorded that the rent charged was £9 per annum. The premises now somewhat different in character are owned by Barclay's Bank.

Opposite above: Sports days were always eagerly awaited. Here at Easington we have a line up of five young lady contestants in the egg and spoon race. The adult events usually offered very attractive prizes for the winners, clocks appear to have been a favourite item on offer, and of course for some events a trophy would be given.

Opposite below: Tea on the lawn at Easington. This is obviously a family occasion with even the baby of the family included. Our forebears loved this type of alfresco gathering, perhaps because they could entertain more people than would have been practical indoors. Note the typical cobbled building, it is thought this photograph was taken at the old Easington windmill.

This is a fine view of Easington village square with the old church elevated on a mound. The earliest part of All Saints Church are thirteenth-century. In the graveyard there are numerous features of interest to the historian, including a memorial to two sisters who were tragically killed when their hair became caught up in a millstone whilst the windmill was grinding corn. Like many villages in the area, cobble stones were widely used as an early and available building material, taken mostly from the local beaches. Some of these cobblestones can be clearly seen above in the wall to the left.

The village of Easington lies on the southern end of Holderness, on that tapering strip which leads down to Spurn and the Humber Estuary. All Saints Church is the central feature of the village, the tower of which can be seen to the left. The impressive thatched structure is one of the few original remaining tithe barns in the country. This immense structure, which still stands as a barn, dates from the fourteenth century, beneath the thatch is a skeleton of huge timbers and an earth floor.

A formal portrait study of Mr. Carter Stringer and his wife Rachel who lived at Bumble Bee Farm at Holmpton, during the early part of the twentieth century. Bumble Bee Farm later became West Farm, and along with Manor Farm and North Farm was owned by a Mr. Herd.

Bumble Bee Farm is typical of the type of farmhouse found throughout the region. Some of the windows have been blocked, possibly in the days of the iniquitous window tax. The little girl is Rachel, the young daughter of Mr. and Mrs. Carter.

There are numerous spellings recorded for the village of Hollym. Holam, Holeym, Holoyme and Halym are the recognised ones, which are all translated as meaning 'homestead near the hollow', and are said to be Anglian in origin. As the above scene conveys, with the cattle grazing by the roadside in the charge of the two men with sticks, like the rest of Holderness it was, and still is, an agriculturally dominated area. St. Nicholas Church can be seen in the distance, it was built in the sixteenth century, being restored around 1725 and rebuilt in 1814.

Patrington Haven Primitive Methodist Chapel where the people have gathered for the unveiling of the War Memorial for those villagers who gave their lives in the Great War of 1914-18.

Left in charge! Two young men 'tent' the cattle in there shadow of the dominant St. Wilfrid's Church at Ottringham.

The village of Welwick in south east Holderness, can boast no stately home or imposing building, but having changed little over the last two hundred years has a charm all of its own. It has a dubious claim to fame as being the birthplace at Ploughland Farm of John and Christopher Wright, two members of the infamous Gunpowder Plot. The attempt by a Catholic motivated group to destroy King James I and the Houses of Parliament when it opened on 5 November 1605. The brothers were killed in the ensuing fight following the discovery of Guy Fawkes in the cellar. The scene above is around the turn of the twentieth century and shows the village inn, the Coach and Horses and a few interested inhabitants who have turned out for the photographer.

Thorngumbald, was, in the days of the Domesday Book called Torne. This was enhanced by a Baron Gumbald who resided in the area, giving the present name. Like most of Holderness it depended on agriculture for its economy, and stands on the coast road between Hull and Withernsea. The two men going about their business, have almost certainly posed for the benefit of the photographer.